CATHOLIC PERSPECTIVES

Abortion

by
John Garvey
and
Frank Morriss

THE THOMAS MORE PRESS
Chicago, Illinois

Acknowledgment: The Chapter entitled "Abortion and Law" originally appeared in slightly different form, in *U.S. Catholic*.

Note: Translation of the *Documents of Vatican II* in Part Two are Copyright The National Catholic News Service and are used here by permission.

ISBN: 0-88347-100-0

CATHOLIC PERSPECTIVES

Abortion

PART ONE

by
John Garvey

INTRODUCTION

THE ISSUE of abortion is one which evokes such strong emotions, so rapidly, that the possibility of objective consideration seems ruled out from the start. In fact, some people would maintain that the idea of objectivity about abortion is obscene, just as it would be obscene to try to be objective about genocide. From this point of view, objectivity is a wrong thing, too sedate a perspective to bring to something as outrageous as abortion.

But this view is met head-on by another, which is just as powerfully felt. In this alternative view, those who oppose abortion are part of a pattern which for millenia has held women in bondage to the way a male-dominated society views their bodies and their pregnancies. To people who feel this way, words about the rights of the unborn and the sanctity of human life look like smoke-screens, ways of hiding the real issue, which is the right of women to determine what happens to their bodies and their lives.

As long as each side refuses to hear and respect the concerns of the other—as long, that is, as each side sincerely believes that the word "murderer" or "oppressor" best characterizes the opposition—the possibility of a reasonable consideration of the issue is remote.

I should, beginning this, state my own position. I am opposed to abortion because it involves taking life. I believe that a society which sees abortion, or any other life-taking, as a practical option (in this case an extreme form of contraception, not really more difficult than any other extraction, morally) is in deep trouble.

However, I believe that the legal arena may be the worst possible place in which to argue this issue. I believe—for reasons which I hope to make clear—that to seek through law an absolute prohibition of abortion will, in the long run, hurt the Christian argument against abortion more than pro-abortion propaganda possibly could. I also believe that to characterize those who believe that abortion should be an option as "murderers" is wrong—not only because it isn't kind or polite to talk that way; it isn't even accurate.

The problem of abortion involves more than either side seems willing to admit. It concerns our definition of what humanity means, what we believe about being alive, how we feel about the degree of control people should have over what happens to them, the relationship of law to this control, and what the relationship of religion is—or should be—to law.

In other words, this is an issue which involves whole complicated layers of our relationship to culture, society, and religion, and involves them in complications which go beyond abortion. And where this issue moves us beyond itself, the result is a consideration of the role of Christians in a world which is not necessarily designed for their comfort, a world in which the desire of women for abortion tells us something as critical as our own opposition to abortion.

Abortion and all of the responses it evokes may serve as a reminder that Christianity involves much more than a set of rules. It is a single-minded vision of what human beings are called to be, and it calls us not to consolation or easy answers, but to a vocation which will lead us not only to oppose abortions; it will also lead to other oppositions and discomforts. If it does not do this it is a reduction, a deathly compromise. My hope here is to clarify the issue of abortion by placing it in the wider Christian context. The effort is dedicated to humane, open-minded people on both sides of the issue.

I

ON ABSOLUTES

There is a modesty about the refusal to make absolute statements which can in some people be a genuine commitment to finding the truth; but the person who says flatly, "I don't believe in absolutes," is foolish: what statement could be more absolute than that one? The thing that has to be done in any talk about absolutes is first of all to say what we mean by an absolute; and if there is such a thing, to show how we are related to it, in speaking and acting.

This sounds very abstract, but it isn't, in application. If, for example, I believe that your right to liberty is absolute—that is, a thing which is essential to what you and I are about—I will behave in a manner quite different from the one I would exhibit if I regarded your liberty as less than central. At the same time, my definition of what "freedom" or "liberty" means may go through all sorts of changes as I try to get at whatever it is I find important about this admittedly difficult thing, freedom. No single one of my statements matters as much as the direction they tend towards. More importantly, I will certainly defend your freedom, if it is threatened, more vigorously than someone who believes freedom to be an expendable thing.

There is a clear direction implicit in Catholic moral theology where it deals with the life of the unborn child. It is not only in favor of regarding that life as worthy of some respect, but it makes a comparison—rightly—between that undeveloped, potential life and our own. In his good essay, "An Almost Absolute Value in History" (in *The Morality of Abortion,* Harvard, 1970), John Noonan writes that in traditional Catholic moral theology, "life even of the innocent was not taken as an absolute. Judgments on acts affecting life issued from a process of weighing. In the weighing, the fetus was always given a value greater than zero, always a value separate and independent from its parents. This value was crucial and fundamental in all Christian thought on the subject and marked it off from any approach which considered that only the parents' interests needed to be considered." For this reason abortion was considered permissible in certain extreme circumstances—ectopic pregnancy, for instance, or in the case of a cancerous uterus. The debate today is not so much over what constitutes a sufficiently extreme circumstance, or whether the traditional Catholic definition is too restrictive; it is rather over the fact that abortion proponents never seem to give the fetus "a value greater than zero."

Catholic opponents of abortion are often accused of trying to force others to accept a religious opinion, namely, the belief that the fetus is human. There is indeed something religious in this belief, as we shall see, but those who argue against it ignore an essential consequence of believing that fetal life is human. If my belief that fetal life is human is sincerely held, and I believe that human life deserves protection, then I may not simply relegate my belief to some broom closet with "religion" written on the door. If a cannibal were to defend his behavior on the grounds that his intended dinner was not really human, and that in trying to rescue his meal I was interfering with his freedom by imposing my religious views upon him, I think we would seek a hole in the argument.

The other argument most frequently heard against opposition to abortion is intellectually a much better one; it also brings us closer to the idea of the absolute, and the question of a religious definition of what it means to be "human." That is the argument that a definition of human life and when it begins is extremely difficult. Abortion opponents sometimes find this hard to understand. There is no doubt that life begins at conception. Cells begin to divide then;

you have a genetically unique entity following conception, containing the code for what that person will be all his or her life. This unique, developing life is certainly in the process of becoming whatever it is we call a human being. Unless it is interrupted, it will be born, and grow up, and die. It will learn to count, hum, lie, love, tell jokes, daydream, and lust; it will be moved to tears, prayer, and anger; how could this life— which certainly begins the process of becoming whatever it will become, uniquely, at conception—not be human? Those who oppose abortion are baffled by people who cannot see the humanity of the fetus.

Their opponents come at it differently. They do not find it easy to define what being human is. Is it merely a unique genetic code? Is it in cell division that humanity lies? There must be more to it than that. There is no evidence that, moments (or even days and weeks) after conception, this life is capable of knowing, caring, understanding, forming relationships, loving, or any of the rest. If humanity is more than mere physical subsistence, it is permissible to question the humanity of this life. And it certainly seems clear that it would be less dreadful to kill life at this stage than to kill someone who could understand that he or she was being killed. To say "abortion is murder" is preposterous.

So one side faces another, across an appar-

11

ently unbridgable gap, each refusing to believe that the other is sincere. You know in your heart of hearts that you are taking human life, says one side. You know that isn't your real concern, says the other; you want to oppress women by forcing them to bear children against their will.

The real issue here is, of course, the definition of human life; and it is here that a certain religious argument does enter the picture. The person who believes that human life begins at conception sees human life as a given, as something that comes with simply being alive; and life itself is seen as given, a gift. The value of life is, from this point of view, objectively a real thing, whatever is thought of it. The belief that human life is in itself of value implies a sense of the sacred.

Those who are willing to overlook the possible humanity of the fetus do so because they believe that humanity has to do with a certain recognizable, definable quality. Our humanity has to do not with anything given to us, but with the relationships we form. In a sense, we confer value and humanity on one another; it doesn't adhere to us, nor is it given from outside. We give it, by valuing and loving one another.

These two points of view are irreconcilable. My sympathies are with the first. The second places the whole burden of what it means to be human on what it means to think about being

human—it makes everything depend upon defi-
nitions *we* give, and rules out any sense of
mystery or sacredness. These are, of course,
religious considerations. As such they should, in
the opinion of secular society, be limited to a
particular sphere.

There is a dark side to defining human life. It
has usually been done in order to limit or elimi-
nate life. Slaves, in much of American history,
had their relative human worth defined. In many
societies the value of female life or old life was
defined as less important than the value of male
life. The most dreadful modern example is, of
course, that of Nazi Germany: Jews, gypsies,
Slavs, homosexuals, and political dissidents
were, in varying degrees, expendable. Unless we
are trying to get rid of life, we are usually content
to leave its definition alone and deliberately
open-ended: who can say what human beings are
fully capable of becoming? If we had a genuine
reverence for life, our inability to define its
beginnings would not lead us to be easy about
taking it, at any stage of development.

But of course this cuts both ways. One cannot
on the one hand say that life is given a sacredness
which human beings may not violate in the
womb, and then say that the murderer has "for-
feited his right to life." If that sacredness is part
of being human, if the phrase "the sanctity of
human life" is not mere rhetoric, it is to be found

as much in a murderer as in a baby. The murderer may have obscured that sacredness in himself, but he cannot forfeit it, as if it were a prize or had anything at all to do with his decisions. Similarly, the person who finds abortion a terrible thing, but was less bothered by napalmed children in Vietnam, apparently regards *only* pre-natal life as sacred.

It is not quite right to say that "life even of the innocent was not taken as an absolute." What was not absolute was the prohibition on taking even the life of the innocent; but for the Christian an absolute value has been placed on every life by the death of Christ. "What you do to the least of the brothers, you do to me," applies not only to the fetus. The least of the brothers is, almost by definition, the one we least want to have around us, or take responsibility for.

The Catholic tradition with regard to abortion is very much like the mainstream of conservative Catholic tradition with regard to capital punishment and war. It may be done in some cases, but the case must be extreme and the results must always be so much weighted in the direction of the good that the evil is tolerable. (An extreme of this position, found on the Catholic right, is that the evil to be tolerated is, because necessary, not really evil; it may, of course, be unpleasant, but there is a stoic pleasure in enduring the unpleasant for the sake of what is higher. We have had to bomb the orphanage, torture the prisoner, kill the deserter, execute the murderer, ah well. All part of the burden we bear as Christians. God knows, it hurts. . . .)

Because of the value that Christ's death has placed on all human life, we should not speak too easily about "necessary evils." Some terrible things, including killing, may in some circumstances seem to be necessary; but the evil involved should not be glossed over on that account. The problem with (for example) the Christian defenses of the possibility of just warfare is that they were never used to condemn any war. More frequently, they excused the acts of the warmakers.

This is not to say that the search for exceptions to the Christian bias in favor of nonviolence makes no sense. To say "killing is wrong" invites the response "always?" And it should. It is not at all the same thing to kill someone for pleasure, because you want to hear the screams, and to kill someone in self-defense. It is similarly not the same thing to kill in self-defense, and to kill another in order to save a third party, where great personal risk is involved for you. At least, it is not the same at one very important level— that of your own subjective guilt or innocence, a level at which intention is all-important.

But there are issues beyond personal guilt and innocence which matter at least as much to the

way we live together as our individual responsibility for any activity. One of them is the result
of our act. To put it coldly, it doesn't matter to
the dead person whether I enjoyed the killing or
not, or even whether the death was intended. The
napalmed child is understandably not concerned
with the intention of the soldier at the easier end
of the deal. Whatever my intention, the person at
the other end of my intention is dead. How guilty
I may or may not be is, perhaps, a question to
take up with my confessor. But beyond this,
something has happened, and some account
must be made of the fact; some witness to the
gravity of the action must be made, as it was during the first Christian centuries, when people
who had killed (even in self defense) fasted from
the eucharist for years.

An approach to moral action which is too in-
dividualistic leaves out the defilement we feel
when we are involved, even unintentionally, in
terrible things. When we watch the agony of
Oedipus we know in some part of our soul that
he is right to feel defiled for murdering his father
and for sleeping with his mother, even though he
is, at the merely personal level, innocent of those
acts. His deeds and their consequences have
marked him, and their weight can't be brushed
aside.

We could think more clearly about these things if we could develop once more a sense of the tragic. It isn't a sensibility confined to Greeks, or a Western thing. The Hopi people—generally pacifist in their dealings with others—once fought a fierce war for survival. The hero of that war, the one who had done the most killing was so filled with a sense of guilt and dread for what he had done that he asked the elders of the tribe to pray over him, to exorcise the evil he had been responsible for bringing into the world. I find this non-Christian tale of a person who could know, even as a hero, that his deeds were evil, a more inspiring thing than the efforts of moral theologians to justify violations of the mystery at the heart of the Incarnation. There can be no greater violation than a deed which denies the holiness of human flesh by killing it. If one feels forced to kill, there can be no more appropriate gesture than mourning, or maybe exorcism. The worst thing of all is to make excuses, to find religious justification for having offed one of the least of the brothers.

What we intend is, putting it mildly, only part of the picture. The lessons of environmental pollution are to the point here. No one ever intended directly to poison air and water; the intention was increased production, etc. But intentions were beside the point. We now have poisoned air and water and land, because of things we did not know, or ignored. Our intentions had little to do with the process.

I am afraid that we are beginning to see the results of a too-individualistic moral theology now. A society in which the majority of people have been willing to lay claim to the word "Christian" as a description of their religious belief offers the world a fair facsimile of imperial Rome, dressing the spectacle up a bit with born-again bumper stickers. Like Rome we hold sway over much of the planet, militarily and economically. And like the pagan Romans, we would like to deny that this fact is religiously important: religion is personal, doesn't touch the way things work, the systems that make people move and jump and twitch and die. If there is any hint that abortion may be part of the pattern which has offered us the neutron bomb, let's not let it out. Let us separate abortion from this web of death, make it a simply moral issue which can be reduced further to a legal issue. Separate it from the rest of the sickness which is killing us, slowly—or so we hope; slow death gives whatever rules us more time. That's what I'd push, if I were the devil in charge of moral issues.

II

ABORTION IN CHRISTIAN HISTORY

The history of Christian opposition to abortion is an important consideration in any discussion of the issue. If, for example, this is a comparatively new concern, its importance for Christians can be understood as a limited and maybe narrow thing, like the momentary worry over evolutionary theory. (This is, of course, not applicable to fundamentalists, for whom history and tradition are absolutely unimportant; their "literal" reading of the Bible shows how drastically unimaginative and unappreciative our definition of literacy has become.)

If religious opposition to abortion were merely recent—or, if ancient, could be read simply in terms of anti-feminism—it could be judged as a less than central Christian issue, a matter of shifting discipline and societal mores. If, however, Christian opposition to abortion is not only ancient, but has rather centrally to do with the attitude of Christians to the society in which they have a function involving participation and prophecy, cooperation and witness, then it can't be so easily dismissed.

There is a danger in using Christian history to illustrate the rightness of an argument, and it must be pointed out here. There have been enough bad things done sincerely in the name of Jesus Christ to make his name suspect. Given the range of possibilities, it is easy for a Christian who wants to make almost any point to look at a choice period of Christian history and find a saint, reformer, or theologian, whose conduct and teaching will justify whatever needs justification.

It is here that a sense of tradition as a living thing is necessary. Where a clear direction can be found in Christian thought it might make for discomfort, even outright disagreement—but at least it can be said that the thought represented in that consensus is historically a clear Christian direction. I believe that this clear direction can be found with regard to abortion. I also believe that it cannot be seen in isolation from other Christian pronouncements on the value of human life, including the lives of the poor, criminals, and enemies. I have a bias which I must make clear, given the picking and choosing opportunities we have. My bias is that Christianity has offered the most honest account of itself when it was least entangled with the world—the world being the one John's gospel speaks of as condemned, including the network of cultural prejudice, social assumptions, and all sorts of notions of respectability—and it is most likely to go wrong when it gives the world a justification for whatever it is the world wants to do. There are times when a radical questioning can seem disloyal (churches and nations are equally guilty of seeing questions this way); but saints and prophets have been forced to oppose the idea that one's cause and country are unquestionably righteous.

A view of Christianity which allows it to become alloyed with anything else is idolatrous. Once we are able too easily to equate Christianity with "society's needs" or "correct politics" or "being good Americans" we are in direct danger of using the gospel to support the thing we are most tempted to set up "in the holy place," the idol of Americanism, anti-Americanism, liberal or conservative or radical values, or whatever else we would rather believe in.

But what about the use of the structures society offers (the law and the courts, for example) to do what really is important? Admitting the danger of being co-opted, would it be wrong for Christians to use the courts to oppose slavery? Granting that Christian's allegiance to government must never be absolute, is it wrong for Christians to use the law? History can help us here, because if we can find some helpful direction in Christian history (especially that period during which Christianity was a new idea) we might have some help in thinking about these things.

* * *

The world which Christianity first confronted was familiar with abortion.* The Jews opposed it, and it was considered curious by sophisticated Romans that the Jews refrained from aborting children, even after wills had been drawn up, making new offspring unwanted complications. John T. Noonan points out the place of children in the New Testament: Jesus brings children to himself, to be blessed, and holds them up as examples to the rest of us. The infancy narratives say that what was in Mary's womb was holy, and Luke writes of John "leaping" in Elizabeth's womb at Mary's greeting. But more specifically, Paul in Galatians condemns *pharmakeia,* the occult use of drugs (literally, "medicine"), a word which was frequently used to describe abortifacient drugs.

* The historical references in this chapter come for the most part from two excellent, and finally differing, books, *Abortion: Law, Choice, and Morality* by Daniel Callahan (Macmillan, 1970), and the essay "An Almost Absolute Value in History" by John T. Noonan, in *The Morality of Abortion,* edited by John Noonan (Harvard University Press, 1970).

The early Christians placed abortion in the same category as homicide. For example, an ancient Syrian writing, *The Didache* (it dates from no later than 100 A.D.) uses Paul's word, *pharmakeia,* in its list of things to be avoided. It goes on to say: "You shall not slay the child by abortion. You shall not kill what is generated." *The Epistle of Barnabas* contains similar language. Clement of Alexandria associates the destruction of the fetus with the destruction of love for humanity. Tertullian condemned abortion, and in the second Christian century a Christian convert, answering anti-Christian allegations that Christians engaged in human sacrifice, argued, "How can we kill a man when we are those who say that all who use abortifacients are homicides, and will account to God for their abortions as for the killing of men. For the fetus in the womb is not an animal" (Noonan, p. 11). In the fourth century Jerome and Augustine made distinctions between the "formed" and "unformed" fetus, but neither allowed abortion, nor did they allow the distinction as a defense for early abortion. St. Basil explicitly rejected the distinction between the formed and unformed fetus as beside the essential point; and John Chrysostom, in an attack on those married men who encouraged prostitutes and mistresses to abort, said: "You do not let a harlot remain only a harlot, but make her a murderess as well'' (Noonan, p. 17).

The ancient Christian opposition to abortion must be cited, because there are a few supporters of permissive abortion laws who assert that Catholic opposition to abortion is fairly recent, and they claim (among other things) that Catholic theologians even permitted it during the first trimester; Aquinas is frequently cited here.

This is simply not the case. These pro-abortion arguments, perhaps reflecting a bit of the old anti-Catholicism which had the pope giving instructions to unquestioning automatons, equate Catholic opposition to abortion with definite papal sentences of excommunication. These *are* late; so is an absolutely authoritarian papacy, and it seems already to be short-lived. This narrow understanding of Catholicism can be put down to ignorance of history. But there is plain sloppy thought behind the idea that a distinction between ''ensoulment'' and ''nonensoulment,'' based as it was in bad biology, is the same thing as permission to abort. The first clear Catholic defenses of the possibility of abortion date from the fourteenth century. They require extreme circumstances (abortion was to be allowed in the case of a diseased uterus or ectopic pregnancy), and they are based on a use of the casuist ''dou-

what it meant to be human which the early Christian apologists believed to be essential. The Jews taught that it was the obligation of the just human being to "love your neighbor as yourself." The Jews were at odds with paganism in many areas, and easy abortion was one of them. Christianity, in claiming a belief in divine humanity, asked Jesus' followers not only to accept the Jewish precept of love of one's neighbor; in addition, Christians must love one another as Jesus had loved them—even to death, if that became necessary. This obligation to assume a divine love of human beings was essential to much early Christian apologetics, which not only opposed abortion, but all shedding of blood, and slavery. Not that there was much demand for insititutional change—the world was probably too near its end for that, in the Christian view. But given the universal demand that we love one another, the consequences were radical enough to distress (or at least amuse) sophisticated Romans. Christians believed that slave men might marry high-born women validly, and that marriages between high-born men and slave women were real marriages, not just concubinages. The Christian bias for nonviolence had nothing at all to do with political expediency. It had nothing to do with the virtue or vice of the opponent, or with the comparative values of the barbarian way of life and the Roman system. Instead, some canons of the Church said that to shed blood—*even in self-defense*—was a deed so grave as to prevent reception of communion for years—years which had to be spent in penance; and murder separated you from communion forever. Killing another human being for any reason at all (his virtue or politics were not even part of the question) was a grave enough matter to demand at least the witness of extreme penance, at most excommunication. Individual guilt and innocence were not as important as repentance for what was obviously an evil event, which allowed evil its edge on the border of the kingdom of Heaven.

This absolute sense of life's sanctity was based, in Christian thought, on the apparently absolute valuation God has given to our lives— to *all* of them. Paul compares our own most generous responses with God's response. He says that while we might in an extreme situation be prepared to die for a good or just person, it was while we were sinners that Jesus was prepared to die for us. That love is—to say the least—startling, and changes the way we must regard our neighbor by dropping his virtue and worth out of the question. As a result, the early Christian ethic with regard to abortion, war, and the status of slaves is radically different from that of the surrounding society. If human life—not life in the abstract but in the flawed particular—is valued to the death by one who shared the life of God without any limit; and if those who recognize this are charged with the work of carrying out the consequences of that love, then. . . .

Then what? Can we regard life in the womb with all of this reverence, as I believe we must, but not the life of the condemned murderer? Or can we regard as expendable the lives of people who happen to be temporary enemies (in politics that is the only kind) of the people in charge of the nation-state which claims to represent us? (Or to be a little more specific: are their subjects worth less, from God's point of view, than our subjects? Should Christians think of "ours" and "theirs" that way, if the kingdom is really among us?) Our lives, all of them, have had their value given, and it is not a limited one.

This radical regard for all human life was never so much at the center of the Christian proclamation as it was in the early years of the church's history, when Christian opposition to abortion was part of a radically different view of life, one which sophisticated pagans (including the great stoic emperor Marcus Aurelius, who persecuted Christians) regarded as a threat to civilized order.

In making such a fuss over slaves, women, the poor, and fetuses, Christians seemed extreme and fanatical to their pagan opponents, who do sound, even at this distance, like reasonable men frustrated by people who will not settle down and accept the way things are. By way of contrast, many early Christian texts (especially accounts of martyrdom) do seem unreasonable and fanatical. Our first mothers and fathers in faith were, it must be remembered, prisoners and criminals. They lost that suspect status only when Christianity began to be an acceptable idea.

Here is the divide: should it have become acceptable?

Is it possible to say that an absolute value has been placed on every life, a value that does not know any limit, including that of death (the resurrection being the great secret) and still live the way we do, accepting the notion that some of us can rightfully hold on to more than we need while others starve, or that the life of a murderer or political enemy is expendable? In any society these ideas are threatening ones. Some people believe that they are essential to Christianity. Others believe that Christianity is about something else. I think the divide is at that point. (I am not on the pure side of this—I own a house, eat well, live quite confortably. But it is certainly not the business of the gospel to shore up my

29

self-regard, swollen as it already is, or to defend my way of life in a world full of refugees.)

Perhaps the division between people who believe that law and Christianity should always work together, and those who are uncomfortable with the idea of coercive support for Christianity, has its roots in a problem which revealed itself early on in Christian history; it is a dialectic between two sorts of Christian, neither of them easily described, and a look at our history will, maybe, serve better than labels here. Labels would only mislead, since each side of this dialectic will look at times conservative, at times radical, at times liberal, all depending upon what is meant by those terms. Some specific examples and directions are more to the point.

Much of the early Christian community expected an imminent apocalypse, and accepted an apocalyptic responsibility. Paul's attitude towards marriage is partially based, apparently, on the belief that it makes little sense to live as if there really would be future generations to worry about, and the strange combination of Christian opposition to slavery and indifference to social revolution has been explained by some historians as a consequence of the same attitude. Why bother to abolish an oppressive structure, if God is about to abolish it himself? However, God's own time for the end of the old order wasn't so clearly defined, it seemed, and as Christianity grew in respectability to become the religion of the empire, the Christian attitude towards society changed. At its worst this change meant that many usable gods were replaced by one usable God. But many humanizing aspects of Christianity entered ordinary social life as a result of this growing respectability. Life was not any longer as cheap as it had been; women, slaves, and children were more important under Christian imperial rule than they had been under paganism.

As Christianity became a ruling religion, life was also no longer valued absolutely, given the threatening possibilities of *that* idea. It is not at all accidental that the first Christian defenses of the possibility of a "just war" happen during the period of ascending Christian respectability and involvement with the empire. On the other hand, it is important to realize that until Christianity began to influence and in some ways come to the defense of the larger culture, the problem of a just war didn't often come up. Similarly, the idea of state and familial ownership of people was made more problematic by the arrival of Christianity into the arena of common politics. The absolute values which the life and death and rising of Jesus illuminate confronted the needs of the world, and an effort was made to build a bridge from the world to that illumination.

Was the effort proper? Or was it a Christian version of building the tower of Babel? (In the words of a Mennonite writer, do we bring the world to Christ, or Christ to the world?)

As Christianity became a cultural influence, it also began to be influenced by the culture; and it became increasingly difficult, after Christianity became the religion of the empire, to separate ecclesiastical from imperial politics. There was a reaction to this: the first monks felt the need to leave a world of assimilated Christianity. There have been objections made to the assertion that monks fled a corrupted form of Christianity, and the objection is good if it is meant to underscore the fact that monasticism was not founded on a negative insight. Monks went *towards* something in the desert (it was the burning bush) and did not leave anything essential. But if the objection to the image of the monk leaving a corrupt world is meant to suggest that the assimilation of Christianity by the empire was a good thing, some questions are raised.

It is certainly true that the Christianization of the empire contributed quite a lot to the empire's improvement in the sphere of social morality. Under growing Christian influence certain harsh pagan laws were dissolved. As several historians have remarked, Christianity led the way from slavery to serfdom. In other words, it may not be so great to be a serf, but it beats hell out of being a slave—and who can argue? But the introduction of assimilated Christianity has a darker side. The Orthodox theologian Sergius Bulgakov, a convert from Marxism, has pointed out the heart of the problem: Christianity at first proclaimed an absolute liberation, but because the end of the world was expected at any moment, no social theory was worked out to accompany the message of the gospel. The consequence was that when Christianity was adopted by the surrounding culture, the church adopted a view of politics which had been formed by pagans, and tried to make it a little bit better.

The problem, then, is this: Christianity can be seen as having two basically different traditions in social thought, both of them concerned with making things better. One involves an effort, informed by the Christian ideal, to make the world better through the use of established channels. Law, conventional morality, public opinion, and other subtle and less subtle pressures are used to make people live as the ideal says they should. This approach assumes that some forms of force and coercion, as means to a good end, are acceptable vehicles of social transformation. The other approach is more radical. It says that the use of *any* force is wrong, that change can be real in Christian terms only where it involves true personal and communal conversion. Coercion of any sort, in this view, may lead to conformity, but not to the changes that matter. A Christianity which reinforces the world's destructive choices, by giving the powers which control the world Christian legitimacy, is a bad thing.

Both traditions have strengths and drawbacks; both have had successes and failures. The successes of the assimilated form of Christianity have been mentioned: it did help to improve things. It is certainly the more practical approach, in the sense that the world will find it more sensible and easy to work with. The drawbacks are also obvious; they include the crusades and the Spanish inquisition.

The drawbacks to the more radical, early Christian approach could be said to come down to its impracticality. It gives very little directly helpful advice. It says, for example, that slaves are equal, and doesn't appreciate the economic and social consequences. It says that Christians must not kill, without offering anything to soften the corollary that this means they will often be killed. Even its successes look like failure: the patriarch who refuses Ivan the Terrible communion is smothered to death, and the people who take the gospel to heart and give away all they have end up being poor. But the witness is clearer.

The time for the assimilated sort of Christianity may already have passed forever. Christendom is dead. We do not now have, and never will have, a Christian country—not, certainly, in the older sense of the word, a country in which most citizens thought of themselves as believing Christians. If we are asked to give witness to the value of life now, how will we go about it? Should the use of law, coercive and limited as it is, be the way we take? Can the issue of abortion be separated from other signs of death's victory—the arms race, the death penalty, our treatment of the old and poor and retarded? And won't addressing all of these issues, as firmly as we should, separate us from the mainstream of our culture? In a later chapter I will try to show why law might be the worst possible way to get a Christian view of life across to those who believe that abortion is permissible. In this chapter I have tried to show that Christian opposition to abortion is ancient, but that it was tied in to other equally radical beliefs, which together make up one witness on behalf of life. That witness was weakened where Christianity became powerful in a worldly sense; it is weakened now, when it is reduced to questions of law, and when abortion is separated from other life and death issues. They are just as essential to Christianity. It is significant, in this connection, that when King Vladimir, the first Christian king of Russia, was converted, his first acts were to abolish the death penalty, and to make sure that bread was given to the poor.

III

ABORTION AND THE LAW

The issue of abortion frequently is presented to us as if there were only two alternatives. The first is that a woman has the right to choose an abortion, and therefore there should be few if any restraints placed upon abortion. The second is that because abortion involves the killing of an innocent human being, it should be forbidden under the law. The latter position is the one taken by America's Catholic bishops. A good number of Catholics agree with them.

But of course the issue is not a Catholic issue. Protestants, Jews, and members of no religion at all find our society's drift towards permissive abortion an appalling thing, and many of them have joined in an effort to ban abortion through the addition of an amendment to the Constitution. This is a reaction to supporters of permissive abortion laws, who cite the Supreme Court decision as a sign that nothing can or should be done about abortion anymore, and to political candidates who try to duck the issue by saying that as much as they personally deplore abortion it is now sanctioned by "the law of the land" (as if this were always a sacred thing). In

37

response, those who favor an amendment argue that the Constitution has been amended before for moral purposes; and slavery—an institution whose effects were remedied in part by amendment—was once the law of the land.

I can understand this position but I believe it is misguided. I am opposed to a constitutional amendment to ban abortion. I am opposed to it *not* because I think it is a woman's moral right to choose abortion. I am opposed to it because it will make for bad law, and in the long run it will hurt the anti-abortion cause. If I thought it would reverse the trend towards a life-denying society, I would be for it. I don't think it will; I think it will have the opposite effect.

Laws made by human beings are not absolute things. They are means to an end, and the end is an orderly society. In a common-law system like ours this means that the law tends to follow the society's own notions about what an orderly society requires.

Some of those requirements are obvious. In the United States, China, Sweden, and the Soviet Union, all legal systems agree that murder, rape, and theft are dangers to society. As different as they are in other respects, these societies understand that the toleration of these destructive kinds of behavior will lead to the destruction of society.

So it is not quite true that "you cannot legislate morality." The phrase is a ringing one, but it shows itself as a half-truth the minute you try to define what you mean by morality. Certainly the law which forbids murder, rape, or theft is a legislation of morality, even if it is the roughest, broadest, most necessary kind of morality. The point is not that morality cannot or should not be legislated, but rather that the *purpose* of law is not the legislation of morality, even though legislation which involves morals sometimes becomes necessary to insure the social order which is law's first concern.

Law does have a moral function besides this ordering one and that is justice. This is the point at which the anti-abortion amendments appear to make sense. Is it not, after all, just to insure the life of an innocent person? Beyond the rather brutal considerations involved in keeping a society from falling apart there are the more delicate kinds, which involve justice, a virtue which transcends the merely necessary and includes society's best hopes for itself. A society so willing to be callous towards its unborn children, a society which has already revealed its callousness towards the old and the poor, is in need of restraints which might conceivably halt its drift towards a vicious, self-centered individualism. Proponents of an anti-abortion amendment quite rightly reject this drift, and they see the amendment as a last-ditch effort to halt a frightening decline the society as a whole seems to have taken.

I agree with the intention. I don't believe that the law is the instrument with which to achieve it. Let me make my discomforts clear.

During a Mass I attended recently a prayer expressed the hope "that our Constitution will again recognize the sanctity of every human life." I couldn't join in the response; language should never be used so carelessly. Our constitution has never recognized any such thing, and there is no sense in talking about recognizing the sanctity of life "again," as if it were once recognized. Slaves were for a long time less than sacred, and according to the most recent Supreme Court decisions on the death penalty (at least the old boys are consistent in their insensitivity) the lives of those on death row are not sacred. The words of the psalm apply: "Put not thy trust in princes . . ." or in courts of law or any coercive authority. At best the courts can be depended on to reflect the better standards of the society which puts them into power; at worst they will reflect the prejudices of a significantly powerful slice of that society.

And that is the beginning of my point. It is a second definition of morality, one which remembers where the word came from. It comes from the Latin *mores,* meaning *customs.* There is nothing necessarily absolute or good about a custom but there is something weighty about it. That weight pulls common law behind it, for better or worse. An example of the way this works is prohibition. There was enough prejudice against drinking to get it added as an amendment to the Constitution, one which later had to be repealed. It was forced into the Constitution by people who were sincerely convinced that they were right, that God was on their side. As a happily drinking believer I don't believe He was, but moral correctness had nothing to do with the success of the amendment in the first place or its repeal in the second. What worked here was the simple fact that enough people opposed the prohibition of alcoholic beverages to make it a national problem while the amendment was in force, by creating a massive criminal industry which met the desires of those who disagreed with the moralists. Eventually those who opposed the amendment made it clear that society could not bear the costs involved in forcing compliance with such an unpopular law.

The tension between the camps staked out on either side of the abortion issue is in large part a tension between the two functions of law in society. Law does on the one hand enforce commonly accepted morality (such as "thou shalt not kill within the borders except with state permission") and to that extent it is a kind of meager guardian of the country's moral life. On the other hand, it can do no more over the long haul than reflect the actual moral perceptions of the country.

This country is a pluralistic society, made up of many people with many values sharing one territory, and the only way we manage to survive together is eventual consensus. What is sacred to one community is not necessarily sacred to another. The consensus we arrive at includes and excludes values at the same time. I am not arguing that the values included or excluded are good, or that they are bad, or that the ones we end up with will be the ones which protect what our own community knows to be holy. I am saying that it is not a moral process; it really never was, except where morality became a social necessity.

If it is a social necessity to see abortion stopped—and I believe that it is, in an ultimate sense—that must be *shown* before it can be enforced; it must be clear to a great majority before it can be effective law.

But, depending on the polls you read, a slight majority or a great minority of the people of America favor making abortion legal. Attitudes have changed drastically during the past decade. Abortion was once considered not only criminal but shocking, and an abortionist was looked upon not merely as a lawbreaker but as a sleazy betrayer of the doctor's calling, an exploiter of the misery of women. Now abortion is considered a more or less acceptable thing, and it is regarded in a number of ways—as a tragic necessity by some, or as a simple extraction by others. In either case the abortionist is seen as a doctor who responds to consumer demands. This is the current position of most Americans, or almost half of us, depending on whom you read.

Any amendment passed in the face of such contrary thinking will not stand for long. Abortions will continue if the Constitution is amended to forbid them. The sole change will be that they will be done despite the law. We might hate the fact, but there simply is a great demand for abortions now, as there was a demand for liquor during the Prohibition era, and if it is not satisfied legally it will be satisfied illegally. Society has moved in that direction, and there is no going back from it at this point, not to the degree that would be necessary to make law an effective medium for underscoring opposition to abortion. There are not enough people who oppose it to make law work effectively.

It is important here to see how the pro-abortionists managed to succeed. They did not begin crudely, by demanding that the Constitution be amended to permit abortions. Instead, the process was one of taking advantage of the prevailing mentality, molding it through educational efforts rather than coercion, until there was a climate which enabled the Supreme Court to act as it did in permitting abortions.

If the opposition to abortion focuses its energy on the law, putting all of its hope into what is, after all, a coercive mechanism, it will find that a pro-life position collapses when the law it has pinned its hopes on collapses. With as many people favoring legalized abortion as opposing it, give or take a few percentage points, there are bound to be immediate and powerfully concentrated efforts to have an anti-abortion amendment repealed, if it ever succeeds; and they are almost certain to win. A reasoned discussion of abortion will end where coercion begins. The sympathies of people will be turned towards those women who will be seen as oppressed by a bunch of celibate males.

And that is the tack that will be taken. It is easier to feel sorry for a pregnant, unmarried teenager than for a bishop.

Think too of the fact that you can reasonably discuss alternatives to abortion with a woman who feels that she has a choice. Threaten her with law, hang jail over her head, and you will not stand a chance of winning her sympathy.

Many former supporters of permissive approaches to abortion are having second thoughts, not so much about the laws as about the life involved—and that is, or ought to be, our primary concern. The case of Dr. Nathanson (who resigned as head of an abortion clinic after years of pro-abortion activity, because he realized the tragic fact that he had involved himself in the taking of life) is one famous incident. There are others, including a growing uneasiness among feminists about their attachments to an issue which can turn ugly, so easily, for such obvious reasons; and in the pages of some left-liberal magazines there is an association of anti-abortion positions with non-violence. The point is not that the whole problem is about to clear up, only that it is not simply a matter of *us* versus *them*. This is a moment in the shifting moral climate of our age which those who oppose abortion could work with. But it will end the moment the law is brought in to make abortion impossible.

My fear, finally, is that the pro-life movement will fail the moment it succeeds. By concentrating its efforts on a constituional ban it will fail, because the immediate consequence will be a flowering of organized crime, intelligent opposition, a continuing drift towards anti-life attitudes, and finally repeal. And after the repeal, the whole of the anti-abortion movement will look to our children the way the Women's Christian Temperance Union—which also put most of its eggs in the legal basket—looks to us: cranky, funny, old-fashioned, and hopelessly out of touch with reality.

IV

CONCLUSION

The issue of abortion will be with us for some time to come. Christian opposition to abortion will continue to baffle and irritate those who cannot understand our belief that life's value is not something to be determined by human beings. Trying to get the message across will not be easy; maybe it can't be done.

But it certainly will not be done if our indignation over life-taking is confined to pre-natal life. All life is sacred—including the life of the criminal and the enemy. The person who opposes abortion vehemently, but accepts capital punishment, the arms race, and the necessity of total war is not at all an effective witness on behalf of life. It may be distressing to have to face these things squarely, but the fact is that the way our society is currently structured is insane; it is a deathly insanity, and abortion is only one of its symptoms. Abortion is, as all of its opponents agree, a sign of something deeply wrong in society. But there are many other signs, and an effective Christianity will try to be clear about all of them.

Finally, it is a religious issue. But we should

not allow the world's definition of religion to influence our own. Ancient Rome found Christianity and Judaism irritating for their insistence that religion was not just part of life, but a commitment involving all of life. In a spiritually indifferent culture, this means that we will not fit in—that isn't our work. Our work on behalf of life comes down, ultimately, to living out the consequences of Jesus' most difficult words:

Love one another, as I have loved you.
Whatever you do to the least human being, you do to me.

CATHOLIC PERSPECTIVES

Abortion

PART TWO

by
Frank Morriss

There is a Catholic doctrine on abortion—one discernible and definable. It is recorded in the historical record of tradition, theological argumentation, and canonical and magisterial (*magister,* teacher, i.e., official teaching) statements.†

But before we proceed, it is important to understand that the Catholic stand today is the same viewpoint long held by all the Western world, once known as Christendom. That view prevailed everywhere till, roughtly, the ending of the first quarter of the Twentieth century.* It was expressed or implied in the teaching of every

---

† = See Appendix

* The approval of abortion, May, 1978, by the Italian Senate is of considerable significance. It shows how an evil may enter society when the influence of the Church over its members is lessened. And it shows how necessary it is to have a Church that does not establish its doctrine by human desire, but by the message given it by Christ and the Commandments of Christ's heavenly Father. The approval came despite what the Church insisted is the duty of government—to act within the ambience of the natural law and to prohibit the intrusion into culture and society of moral evils that strike at the very heart of human nature itself. If a notion of government contrary to that is not to establish itself permanently and universally (that is, a permanent and universal absolutism) then the Church's view—once honored by all Western nations—must once again prevail. Abortion can well be the final test case between true liberty and absolutism, whether of the majority or the minority will. Either truth will prevail, or the claim of humans to *establish* truth.

Christian religion—teaching being only a gentler term for doctrine; and when, with the final triumph of secularism the idea of religious doctrine began to fade, it survived in the belief of a majority of all Christians (and I have no doubt many Jews, as well), in the expression of Western law, and the universal practice of the respectable medical profession.

This is all a matter of ordinary scholarship and living memory, and hardly calls for a mustering of evidence in support of it. Before roughly 1930 no major Christian denomination admitted the permissibility of induced abortion. Before the 1960s no law of any jurisdiction of Western civilization considered the acceptability of legally approved artificial abortion, though some statutes admitted as a defense against penalty a doctor's claim to having acted honestly and professionally to save a mother's life.

In other words, the Catholic doctrine is what the universal belief of all the West held until very recent years. If the Catholic doctrine is now considered at odds with the law or with majority opinion (the latter point never authentically established), or with so-called "rights" or "liberty," it is because those holding such "enlightened" views have changed, have abandoned a centuries-old point of law and conscience.

The Catholic doctrine has stood unchanged, despite the uneducated argumentation of some to the contrary (based upon a misunderstanding of legitimate changes in discipline and penalty concerning the evil itself). Either the new viewpoint (that tolerates, or approves, or applauds abortion) has suddenly become right, or the older viewpoint is still right. Either the traditional viewpoint of all the Western world has been suddenly found wrong or has been evaporated by an evolutionary concept of truth, or the new viewpoint is wrong. It is the burden of what follows to uphold the thesis that the traditional viewpoint, that taught by the Catholic Church and accepted by all of Western civilization until recently, is the viewpoint demanded by truth and also by the very nature and purpose of government and civilization. Contrariwise, the new viewpoint—that of the acceptability of "right" or even desirability of legally approved abortion—is wrong and not only dangerous to the fabric of society, but incompatible with any true concept of authority and law.†

Pre-Christian civilizations were ambivalent about protecting unborn life. In moments of greater philosophic purity, the Greeks insisted it

† = See Appendix

53

not be touched. And so the great teacher Hippocrates demanded of his students that they not help a mother rid herself of the life in her womb.† But where race or nation or clan or citizenship were exalted disproportionately the yet-to-be-born or even the newborn were in jeopardy.

Thus Spartans (as some more primitive peoples do today) destroyed the weaklings, and Roman men might decide that all children conceived after the writing of their will should be denied existence—for not to do so would disturb the property settlement. (That is a neat prefiguring of the modern argument that the unborn should not be allowed to untidy the status quo!) In the pagan civilizations of the mid-East, northern Africa and the East the living were sacrificed to dead idols, as in fact was the case in the Aztec culture overthrown by the Spaniards.

The Jews had Yahweh's command—Kill Not! And this was held by most to apply to the unborn, the "fruit of the womb," a term speaking of something highly good and desirable, a blessing from God.† Childlessness was a curse, and to induce abortion was to make active a curse and mock Yahweh.

† = See Appendix

Apologists of the age of the catacombs facing the wild charge that Christians practiced cannibalism answered that Christians did not even practice abortion (as did the Romans themselves) much less consume babies.† A document that certainly dates well within the living memory of the Apostles themselves and which gives the Apostles' teachings of Christ's own doctrine condemns abortion. That document is the *Didache,* or Catechism of the Twelve Apostles.† It is inescapable, therefore, that the Twelve teachers commissioned directly by Christ felt abortion was outside the pale of the Master's doctrine.

Had not that Master taught that life was central in God's love, and was given not with the intention of death but with the promise of eternal life? The least life was his Father's and is precious in his sight, for he eyes such life more closely than he does each sparrow, whose fall he notes and whose welfare he provides. The sorrow of a mother in the pain of labor is nothing compared to her joy in bringing a human life into the world. The divine Person was present in his mother's womb, having been conceived there by the Holy Ghost. The unborn John the Baptist responds to the presence of Christ in the sanc-

† = See Appendix

tuary of Mary's womb.† The Psalmist had
spoken of the Christ as his God even from the
womb of the mother of that inspired poet. It
takes no distortion to appreciate the basis for the
Didache's absolute rejection of what was a
popular crime among the pagans of the day.

It was clear to the earliest Christians—as it is
clear to the contemporary person faithful to that
original vision—that when the New Testament
speaks of John the Baptist in his mother's womb,
and Christ in his mother's, it is speaking of
human nature in the first case, touched with the
unsurpassed gift of grace while still in the womb,
and the presence in Mary's body of divine-
human nature in the Person of Jesus. *Conception,* therefore, and not just birth is intimately
involved in God's plan both for the propagation
of the species but more so for the increase of
God's kingdom, its population, the existence of
the Mystical Body. That Body actually existed
while Jesus was yet in his mother's womb, and its
greatest Prophet was somehow a member of that
Body while he, John, was still within Elizabeth.

The pristine purity of Mary, freed from sin
from *conception,* undoubtedly reinforced the
Christian respect for life in the womb. The condition of soul begins at conception—for soul is

† = See Appendix

one with human life itself, so that unless one accepts a now discredited idea of vegetative and animal-life stages within the womb one must admit the life that is there is ensouled. True there remains biological and psychological development; but such does not begin nor end with birth and certainly does not alter the nature of the developing being.

All of this, of course, involves philosophy, religion, biology. And it immediately invokes society, culture, law, and the authority that is invested in the two societies—Church and State. Only an appreciation of the full reality of human nature can contribute to a full appreciation of the enormity of abortion. It is the passing of such appreciation that has led some to be able to accept such enormity as commonplace and tolerable.

To help shatter such shocking inhumanity, if it is possible, let us consider a theological point that is seldom mentioned in connection with abortion.

God knows all things—those that are and those that shall be; as well, he knows all that could have been, would have been, or perhaps should have been. He knows the athletic accomplishments denied some youth by accident or premature death. He knows the rejected crown of sainthood that could have been some man or woman's, had they not rejected it for hell. He knows the very persons denied existence by contraception. He knows the great benefits denied civilization by evils, treason, betrayal, ineptitude, cowardice, sloth, dissipation.

Thus, God knows not only *what* is killed in the womb—a knowledge available to us—but He also knows *who* is thus slain. He knows the thwarted destiny of the ones denied birth, the unclaimable sweetness of their lives at every never-to-be moment; the beauty unobtained of their faces and bodies, the stolen desires of their hearts, the denied thrills of their possible attainments. He knows each irretrievable lost moment of their lives, the roles they would have had in history, the feasts and loves they would have enjoyed.

Some may argue that simply a blob of tissue is destroyed when a child is killed in the womb. But if God is who and what believers have always held him to be, with the omniscience we ascribe to him—then each abortion makes a bloody wreck of some masterpiece of God's vision—and only his power to draw good from evil makes such a horror bearable. No one appreciative of God as Creator and Designer can consider the unborn unworthy or not entitled to protection. If a half-finished canvas of Rembrandt or the still-to-be-finished Pieta of Michelangelo would obviously seem worth protecting, though we knew not the attitude of the final work, surely that conceived as a result of God's planning and design is even more worth protecting.

Our environmentalists tell us, with some truth, that in the words of the poet Hopkins we know not what we do when we delve and hew, hack and rack the growing green. Nor do we fully comprehend what we liquidate when we kill an unborn child—what potentiality we destroy, what eventuality we render impossible, what artist, saint, leader we deny the world. But we do know we deny some person—with all a person's distinctiveness—a future in that world, a world we ourselves already enjoy.

I do not mean to deal in purple patches, certainly not for mere emotional effect. But to get the attention of all concerned—which means all humanity—they must understand fully what abortion is, before they will likely consider the less emotional intellectual arguments against it.

It was only through the loss of just such an appreciation of the real meaning of abortion that it returned out of the shadows of paganism. Anyone who heard the recent legislative debates, or who has read the judicial opinions, must have the feeling that nowhere is the full reality grasped, certainly not firmly and securely. All that was considered were shadows of things based on unproved assumptions and unwarranted conclusions. Never was real consideration given to the question: "What is this abortion we are asked to legalize?"

No wonder, then, that the universal resistance to abortion was broken. It was accomplished by losing sight of the reality of abortion itself. Part of what is presented here, therefore, is an effort to deal with the reality, bring it out from its cocoon of soft language, with its wrappings of illogic and poor reasoning.

Prescinding from the theological truth that the sin of abortion can be simply the willing of it, and from the canonical fact that the penalty of excommunication for that sin rests on successful carrying out of the intent—abortion for the purposes of this essay consists of *action or actions contracted for or done with the intention of liquidating life conceived and existing within a mother.* I believe at the moment we can set aside legal niceties about the success of the actions—or where that success is obtained, (whether within the mother's body or after the baby emerges) or indeed whether the attempt might fail and the child might live (an extremely rare but known possibility).

It is the attempt at abortion—the contracting for the actions and the taking of them—that has recently been legalized, and which Catholic doctrine, as I shall attempt to show, teaches should be prevented by what law can be most effective—most anti-abortionists believing that only a Constitutional guarantee of the unborn's right to life can be effective.

The immoral actions which should be outlawed are various. They range from primitive exercises by the mother or insertion of foreign materials into the womb, to more "sophisticated" use of tools that cut or crush the child; caustic liquids that inflict fatal burns; chemicals or hormones that induce the child's premature expulsion from the life-preserving environment—all amounting to an attack of fatal intention and almost always fatal result, upon the unborn.

The Church absolutely forbids to its members all such actions brought directly and immediately against the life within the mother. When the actions succeed, it excommunicates all directly involved—that is, it denies them the comfort of the sacraments and full participation in the Church's life until such time as they seek and obtain the lifting of the penalty. It considers the actions of abortion homicidal, that is aimed at the killing of "man," the generic term for a human being. Legal differentiation of what type of homicide it might be is not germane at this point of the discussion.

What is germane is that the Church teaches the state not only may, but must prohibit such actions for the common good and in fulfillment of its duty to guard rights and prevent violence against anyone.† What type of prohibition would satisfy the Church's teaching will be discussed later. For the moment it should be understood that the Church's social teaching calls for state interference on the side of unborn life and against the attackers, just as it calls for state interference against any attack against the mother's life.

† = See Appendix

Frank Morriss

WHAT IS THE LIFE IN THE WOMB?

There is no need here to go into biological detail about life in the womb. It is good to consider, however, that the various labels for that life given by scientists to mark different points in its development are artificial. Whether or not one wishes to establish a division into blastula, zygote, etc. (a classification we continue even after birth—puberty, senility, etc.) still there is no controversy over *what* life is there. No one holds the medieval idea that it is for a time the life of a vegetable, then of a brute, and finally a human. It is the same *life* that if allowed will one day leave the womb. It is the life that those so destined will give up in advanced years.†

The life begins precisely at the moment the ovum is penetrated by a single spermatozoon, when the ovum is mobile and unattached to the mother, usually in the Fallopian tube. Attachment to the mother will come later, but at that moment is determined what is existing—human life—and also *who* is existing, that is, boy or girl, whether destined to have curly hair or straight, brown, red or black; dimpled or not of chin, a

† = See Appendix

63

nose shaped so-and-so; the type of ear, etc. *To say human life is to say human person.*†

Allowed to do so, this life will become attached to its mother's womb, in order to draw sustenance and to have a special type of "bathosphere," a sack in which it is more or less free moving. It will soon have the features of a human baby, will be able to gyrate, turn somersaults within its mother, suck its thumb. At one stage it will be capable of breathing, should it come upon air, rather than the liquid which is the common intrauterine environment. It has been known to cry within the womb; to smile, to react to touch.

This life exists prior to its attachment to its mother, and is far more—and distinct from—simply a human cell or appendage. It will ordinarily leave the mother's body by natural process, be detached from its connection with its mother, taking oxygen from inhaled air. It will need protective help and specialized environment for a period, nourishment from its mother's body or a substitute, protection against cold, etc. But nothing essential will have happened to it at birth, no change of the life, no mutation or personalization. It is five minutes after birth *what* and *who* it was five minutes before.

† = See Appendix

The idea that somehow it receives a human life at first breath is based on pure fundamental interpretation of Genesis, wherein God breathed life into Adam. But in reality, the only change through breathing is a functional change of the life that was present from conception. It was not dead clay before birth, as was Adam before being given a soul by God.

Left alone, the new-born child will squirm, whimper, struggle to breathe—and perhaps even succeed; but more likely it will gradually lose strength and the life will depart. It will die. What has died? A human being—very young, not yet well developed—but a human being. It is indeed more helpless at that point than when it was in the womb, for then it was in an environment wonderfully designed to sustain its life. Within the womb it must undergo fierce attack if it is to die. Afterward, it may simply be allowed to die. But in both cases it is a death—of what? The answer is obvious. A human has died when the life in the womb is crushed out, burned away— just as a human has died when a baby is denied help to survive.

Argumentation to the Contrary

In order to obtain even a hearing on the acceptability of abortion, those in its favor have had to resort to the illusion that what is in the womb is simply part of the mother. Thus can be entertained the slogan: "Free Us From Attempts to Control Our Bodies," or some such.

Syllogistically the argument is this:

> I may do what I wish with my body.
> But conceived life is part of my body.
> Therefore, I may do what I wish with conceived life.

Let us consider both premises, for if either is faulty the conclusion does not follow.

Morally, one is not allowed to do anything one wishes with one's body. Among the purposes of having a body is not its destruction. The Church teaches, in fact, that what is true of the whole is true of a part. Just as it is wrong to kill oneself, it is wrong to mutilate oneself. It would be gravely sinful for a person out of whim or preference to cut off an arm or ear or put out an eye. One's bodily parts may be sacrificed only for the good of the whole. Diseased organs may be removed, and perhaps even cosmetic surgery aimed at perfecting appearance might be allowed. Otherwise, the body is not under the absolute dominion of its possessor, for it is provided the person by a divine Designer and toward a purpose that is not completely personal or individual.

Nor may one use his or her body as one chooses, without reference to the harm done to others by such use. One could not without moral and undoubtedly legal liability choose to sit down on a chair on which an infant was laid, knowing the child is there and would be injured and probably killed by such action. One could not throw his or her body out a window upon people beneath without, again, being subject to moral and legal penalty.

There is, in fact, a real question as to whether one may indulge himself or herself in a way that is an expense or a major nuisance to others. Syndicated writer Ellen Goodman contributed an interesting column some time ago about the claim of the drinker to drink because—"It's my liver;" or the smoker to smoke because—"It's my lungs;" or the motorcyclist to go helmetless because—"It's my cranium." Ms. Goodman countered with the argument that such things as medical costs, research against cancer, insurance, taxes are involved. Though I cannot quite agree with the application of her thought, still her logic is pertinent here. There is a point at which society, speaking either from the point of morality or civic responsibility, can say that you cannot use your body just as you wish. There are other things involved, other results to be considered.

Now, if such is the case possibly regarding smoking, drinking, wearing helmets or even buckling seat belts—it would seem infinitely more the case in regard to the bearing of children, the future of the race and nation. There is not merely the point of public expense, especially when tax funds are used to provide abortions—but also the question of public good, the attitude that makes society livable and oriented toward justice—a major point that is considered below.

Even—with a wild exercise of imagination— were we to consider the unborn child something of a node, like a strawberry runner, attached to the mother like an offshoot, would that change the moral issue? No species of nature sacrifices the next generation for the temporary benefit of the present one. It would be no more moral or reasonable for women to terminate babies if they were offshoots. The means of reproduction are superficial. The result of reproduction is what is determinative.

(The question of cloning of humans is so theoretical as to not need attention here. But it is interesting to see the concern for "ethics" in this so-called possibility of "laboratory creation."

Such a concern is largely absent in the very real question of terminating "womb creation" conceived in a normal manner—that is, such concern is absent among most pro-abortionists.)

Upholding abortion on the grounds the baby is "part of the mother" is to render abortion the most senseless of all activities. For nowhere outside of man does the parent kill simply for the parent's convenience. Nowhere does nature abort for the shallowest of reasons.

Of course, the first premise of the syllogism is wrong. So no matter how you might argue one's right to control one's own body (and control is an ironic word for killing that takes place to "remedy" the result of uncontrol), it does not follow that you may kill what is in the womb.

I do not know of any biologist or geneticist who argues completely and bluntly that what is in the womb is merely an appendage of the mother. All seem to agree that it is an entity with human life, a life apart from the mother's. Let the mother die, and that human life in her womb will survive a time, and not merely as cellular life (the growth of hair and fingernails) survives. More than once a child has been taken from its dead mother, and has survived and developed into adulthood. Humans are not so created that any mere *part* of them can do so. Artificial wombs move closer and closer to the possibility of survival outside the mother.

And, indeed, in a multitude of tort cases in law the unborn child has been granted damages as an individual, and many cases have been successfully brought in criminal law for injury to the unborn child—even for its murder. The notion that the unborn child is part of the mother is a myth invented simply to uphold what without that myth cannot be considered as anything but reprehensible and well within the public competence to ban.

Human Life But Not Human Person?

Experts, knowing the inadequacy of the claim that there is not independent human life in the womb, but being nevertheless pro-abortion, devise a more sophisticated argument. It is indeed human life that exists; but mere human life is not of overwhelming importance. "Nature" itself aborts imperfect human life. What is of value is the "person," and obviously the fetus is not a person.

Before we analyze that argument, let us point out the incalculable danger of divorcing the concept of person from human life. It creates an artificial and dangerous caste system. The implication is that some human life is inferior, being not "person." It creates "unpersons" as surely as the laws and actions of totalitarian regimes, and just as surely marks such "unpersons" for possible liquidation. True, the argument at the moment is limited to human life in the womb. The fetus becomes an unperson. But having accomplished that, no logic, legal argument or reason remains for not so declaring all who do not fit whatever may be the prevailing view of what it is to be a "person." Black slaves were once ruled by the U.S. Supreme Court to be unpersons, and had that ruling been made in the atmosphere of today's cruelty and contempt for life, the slaves would have been open to possible liquidation.

The argument under consideration here creates an arbitrary and completely un-philosophic definition of person. It draws more from the realm of socio-politics than from philosophy or theology in order to create a definition of person based on function, rather than on metaphysics. It confuses utterly the notion of "personality" with that of "person."

This attitude assumes a measurement to determine the "personness" of life, a measure that is, perforce, subjective, conditioned a great deal by our art and entertainment, by cultural values, but most of all by convenience and self-serving taste. It is a compelling measurement, because it is true there are great personality differences, and our response to others does depend considerably on personality. Personality often determines success, which is a measure of acceptance by others.

There are the sullen, the clodish—those who are in today's vernacular "square." There are chronic non-achievers, misfits. Only the most rigid egalitarians would maintain that differentiations such as this are solely the result of environment. Some seem almost so devoid of the human spirit as to be immoveable objects. What to them are Plato, the swing of the Pleiades, the rift of dawn, the reddening of the rose—to borrow from Edwin Markham's masterpiece poem. They add nothing to any gathering; they move heavily through life, as if in some invisible isolation booth. Contacts between them and the more personable are awkward for both parties.

And, unfortunately, some small degree of such unpleasant "non-personality" seems to afflict almost all who advance in years, so much so that we praise an oldster who is "full of life," who stays "young," and is filled with wit and quickness. But others we pity, as they sink into "second childhood," an ominous forecast of a return to a "fetal state," but one from which there will be no escape by development and a second birth.

If, indeed, "person" is not the equivalent of human life (as I said above, to say person *is* to say human life), then basing rights on personhood will exclude many. If "person" is the equivalent of functioning the way society considers a "person" should function, then both life in the womb and life of the senile, life of the misfits, life of brain-damaged, etc., will be in danger.

The temptation to create the ideal society based on such measurement will be too strong to resist. Indeed, why resist it if that which is admittedly alive, but not possessing the attributes of "person" can be legally liquidated? Does not our law speak of the right of "persons" (Fourteenth Amendment), not those having human life, even though the Declaration of Independence so chauvinistically bases the rights of life, liberty and the pursuit of happiness upon being a "man"—a symbol for the metaphysical reality of having human nature. ("All men are created equal," etc.)

It should hardly need to be said that this idea of the inferiority of some human lives (that is, a basic, or metaphysical inferiority) is all highly un-Christian. The Christian idea of our attitude and regard for others is not based on any such superficialities. We are to love others as we love ourself, the otherness being precisely that they are not the person that is me but another person; they are not like me in "personality," but in nature, in having the same Heavenly Father.

Children disturbed Christ's adult followers. They contributed nothing to the magnitude of events. Like the "Short People" of the recent and outrageous popular song, they just got underfoot and in the way. (The same was true, incidentally, of that persistent little fellow, Zacheaus, whom Jesus honored with a home visit). Christ welcomed them and said it was of such that heaven is thronged, a clear indication that getting to heaven is not achievement, the work of what the world calls "personality."

Christ, we should remember, was "liquidated" (or so His executioners reckoned) because he was a misfit; he was considered of less value than the nation, or the society which set the standards of acceptability in His day.

Child or Mother? Which Shall Live?

It is ironic that some who say the Church takes the unborn child's side against the mother would create a situation at law in which society in effect is always on the mother's side should she choose against the child—and never the other way around.

The truth is that the Church does not distinguish between the value of persons' lives, and indeed insists that no one has the right to make such a distinction. To legalize abortion as it has been legalized in most U.S. jurisdictions is to say that the child's right to life, to possess a powerful defender in the form of law, is completely subordinate to a mother's right to choose against that life. It is therefore to establish a caste system, to differentiate between the life of individuals, and to prevent law from ever taking the child's side.

We are not, of course, speaking here of the natural and anciently recognized right to defend one's life with even deadly force against aggression. But there is no basis for considering the child in the womb, existing there by an action of nature and generally by the free choice of those who engaged in sexual union, to be an aggressor.

We are left, however, with the claim that sometimes the child is a threat to the mother's life, innocent but still by its very presence or the physical demands of a delivery such a threat. Surely we cannot ask that law prevent an abortion in such a case.

Let it be recognized immediately that such conditions are in fact so rare as to be not determinable in any practical discussion of whether we should continue "legalized" abortion. It would be somewhat similar to demanding that a 90-mile speed limit be legalized because under some unlikely circumstance such a speed might save a life; or that shooting persons with curare-dipped arrows be legalized because in one case in a million the curare might act as life-saving medication. No doctor has to give overwhelming weight to the slight chance that carrying a child to term in today's circumstances is going to threaten a mother's life. There is a mathematical risk in giving birth. That is undeniable. The risk in delivering, if necessary, by caesarian section, is barely greater. There is a mathematical risk in almost all we do—even eating a piece of steak or lifting weights or flying a kite. But dangers through infection or uncontrolled bleeding in childbirth have been reduced to the point of extreme rarity.

In other words, the danger to the mother in being denied an abortion is so small as to not be decisive in whether abortion should be legal, a condition where the death of a large number of babies is certain, and wherein medical effort is actually turned against them rather than being exercised in their behalf.

Most proponents of a legal ban on abortion would not object to a return to the legal condition in which a defense would be that the doctor took recognized and necessary medical procedure to save a mother's life, though the death of the infant followed. It is interesting that where such defense was allowed in laws banning abortion it was seldom if ever entered, possibly because it could seldom if ever be sustained in fact.

Allowing such a defense does not have the state do what it cannot properly do—approve of direct attack on the unborn. Nor should any similar argument be allowed as a defense for killing the unborn child simply because it was conceived as a result of incest or rape. In those cases the presence of the child is no more a threat to the mother than if it had been conceived legitimately. Abortion of children conceived by incest or rape is to make them the scapegoat for others' crimes; it smacks highly of revenge, treating the child as if it were a wrongdoer. Such an attitude, to say nothing of its "legalization," is indefensible in any properly functioning society.

Perhaps too few Catholics know that the Church approves the morality of cleansing the woman's body of the seed implanted during assault. As the rapist is an aggressor, so too can his semen be considered such, and can be morally repelled by douching, scraping, etc. This must take place only during the period when medical science can say a conception may not yet have taken place. After that period, when abortion would be likely or certain, the attack would be against an innocent possible child, and therefore could only be immoral.

Though an honest plea of effort to save a mother can be tolerated, the defense of the mother's "medical welfare" cannot be countenanced. Today, with the acceptance of psychology as an equal determinant as to the mother's physical welfare, a mere case of maternal nerves will justify abortion. The merest chance of unfavorable reaction to drugs, to anesthesia, the very morning sickness that is so often an accompaniment to pregnancy—all can be interpreted as an excuse for the mother to consider the child a threat. Indeed, some legal decisions regarding the right of a woman to cosmetic surgery might allow the change in her shape to be considered medically and physically "abnormal."

How many unborn children, could they be

somehow raised to maturity of intellect and will and presented this question—"Would you wish to live if doing so would mean your mother's death?"—how many might answer, "No! Save my mother." But, knowing human nature as we know it—and in view of the rush for abortions against all maternal instinct—we must presume that many, many more unborn, in this imagined situation, would answer, "No—save me, give me my life, even if you must *kill* my mother to do so."

Would the Church countenance a law that would allow a doctor to conspire with an unborn child (in our imagined situation) to kill the mother? Would society accept such a legalized conspiracy?

The abortion law simply reverses the facts, since only the mother can choose. She is mature. A few have heroically said, "Save my child, even if I must give my life." But we know through experience that thousands say, "Take the life in my womb," but almost always without even the excuse that her life is threatened, but for *convenience.* Yet we are told the state and society should not interfere.

There once prevailed a custom whereby the throng in the great Colosseum of ancient Rome could choose life or death for a defeated gladiator. In that case the gladiator might expect some rare outbreak of mercy.

The Supreme Court now plays Emperor for the throng in the Colosseum. It tells mothers that we—the government, the citizenry, the majesty and dignity of law—will turn thumbs down with you if you feel the unborn child must die, for even the slightest reason.

The Catholic Church and, of course, many others, say this must stop. Neither government, law, or civilization can survive such a situation in which the rights of the helpless are ignored, or at least put in extreme jeopardy with the consent of legislatures and courts.

Law under such circumstance has delegated its decisiveness into the care of others, who have replaced it with whim. Society thereby gives itself to the bloody entertainment of the Colosseum, and civilization wears only a masque behind which is either barbarity, or the even worse countenance of sophisticated paganism.

Should Government Ban
Abortion by Law?

There are those, including some Catholics, who would agree with much of what is written above. They will nod approval to the proposition that abortion is evil, call it the result of disordered society, admit to the humanness of what is in the womb, and possibly even accept the argument that human life is the equivalent of personhood. But they will insist it is not proper for the government to interfere in the matter; or will say such moral judgment cannot be imposed by law; or will maintain that it would be bad law because the evil of abortion would not thereby be ended, but would be driven into back-alley rooms with greater risk to the mother's life.

The truly Catholic answer to these objections rests in the fact that the Church has a doctrine concerning government every bit as definite and compelling as its doctrine concerning the sacredness and inviolability of human life. And here again, as regarding the Catholic condemnation of abortion, the Church's doctrine of government was long that of all the West, and was the basis of much common law in defense of human rights. Applying that Catholic doctrine of the nature of government leaves us with only one possibility—the state must declare the illegality of abortion and do its best to prevent its criminal practice.

To understand why this is so we must start with a discussion of government itself. The Catholic Church, virtually alone, continues to insist that government is not the creation of man, but of God. It did not result from some sort of human compact for utilitarian purposes—as Hobbes, Locke, Rousseau maintained—but came into being with man's creation and because of what man is—a social creature destined to live with others of his kind. It is a natural society, not an artificial one, and therefore has a definite and discernible nature, duties, limitations, etc.

"It is clear that the political community and public authority are based on human nature and therefore they need belong to an order established by God. . . ." That statement by Vatican II (*Gaudium et Spes,* III, 2:74) simply repeats the constant understanding of Christianity until the age of rationalism and the so-called "divine right of kings"—i.e., the age of absolutism. It continues with the true and moral understanding of government's origin and orientation which dictate and validate the exercise of all civil authority.

Elsewhere in *Gaudium et Spes* Vatican II is more specific as to the duty of public servants:

" . . . They must take action against any form of injustice and tyranny. . . ."

That farsighted Pontiff, Leo XIII, who almost before its appearance was resisting and refuting the idea of the modern totalitarian state, discussed the duties of the state in his great charter of the rights of workers, *Rerum Novarum* (1891):

It is not right, as We have said, for either the citizens or the family to be absorbed by the State: it is proper that the individual and the family should be permitted to retain their freedom of action, *so far as this is possible without jeopardizing the common good and without injuring anyone.* Nevertheless, those who govern must see to it that they protect the community and its constituent parts; the community, because nature has entrusted its safeguarding to the sovereign power in the state to such an extent that the protection of the public welfare is not only the supreme law, but is the entire cause and reason for sovereignty; and the constituent parts, because philosophy and Christian faith agree that the administration of the State has from nature as its purpose, not the benefit of those to whom it has been entrusted, but the benefit of those who have been entrusted to it. And since the power of governing comes from God and is a participation, as it were, in His supreme sovereignty, it ought to be administered according to the example of the Divine power, which looks with paternal care to the welfare of individual creatures as well as to those of all creation. If therefore, any injury has been done to or threatens either the common good or the interest of individual groups, which injury cannot in any other way be repaired or prevented, *it is necessary for public authority to intervene* (emphasis added).

It indeed was a complaint on this score that made up one of the charges of the Declaration of Independence against George III:

He has refused his assent to laws, the most wholesome and necessary for the public good. . . . He has forbidden his Governors to pass laws of immediate and pressing importance. . . . He has obstructed the administration of justice, by refusing his assent to laws for establishing judiciary powers. . . ."

Substitute the Supreme Court for the "He" and you have a similar exercise of absolutism in the decision prohibiting (or virtually so) any effective laws against abortion. The authors and adopters of the Declaration were, you see, still in the ancient Catholic tradition of law and government, albeit through the interpretation of John Locke, who except for the "compact" theory stated what Cardinal Bellarmine himself had argued concerning government's role and limitation.

When Vatican II includes abortion among the "abominable crimes" against life and a violation of the demand of God that men safeguard life, it becomes abundantly clear that this protection does not simply rest with the individual conscience, but calls into action the responsibility of government.

"Rights, indeed, *by whomsoever possessed,* must be religiously protected; and public authority in warding off injuries and punishing wrongs, ought to see to it that individuals may have and hold what belongs to them" (*Rerum Novarum,* 53—emphasis added).

Although Pope Leo XIII was here speaking specifically of rights or property, organization, religious practice—it follows inexorably that the same teaching applies to the highest right—that of life—against anyone who would take it. There is absolutely no question of the Church's teaching that the state not only can, but must, do all possible to prevent abortion, which violates the rights of the weakest of all.

Pope Pius XI in the encyclical *Quadragesimo Anno* was speaking about economic and labor abuses when he said, "A stern insistence on the moral law, enforced with vigor by civil authority, could have dispelled or perhaps averted these enormous evils." The same must be said about abortion, for it is the most enormous evil of all inflicting society today. If government is morally (that is by obligation of its nature) obliged to act against abuses of working men and women, and even children, how much more is it obliged to act against the final and fatal abuse of the unborn child.

All of the Popes, starting with Leo, condemned the damage to the weak and poor by the utterly free exercise of economics, without interference by the state (Manchesterian liberalism). Many of those abuses were, in fact, ended by such intervention—by minimum wage laws, anti-monopoly laws, laws upholding the rights to organize, controlling working hours, restricting the power of corporations to interfere with workers rights, and, more lately restricting abuse of unions' newly acquired power.

Now, Father Robert Drinan, S.J., as Congressman, and other Catholics who insist on a hands-off policy for the government concerning abortion do not insist on a hands-off policy for the government concerning other matters of social concern. Quite the opposite, certainly in the case of Father Drinan. Yet abortion is now rampant, with legal approval, because the Supreme Court insists that the government's right to protect human life ends at the womb! We have installed the worst kind of *laissez-faire* immorality in an area far more sensitive and important than wages and working conditions. And as the Church did not hesitate to condemn such "freedom," it now does not hesitate to condemn the "freedom" to take unborn human life.

I may scandalize those who misconstrue the First Amendment to mean an absolute separation of state and morality when I say that Catholic doctrine cannot accept such a dichotomy. This brings us to one of the most misleading arguments of all—that any law against abortion would install the Catholic Church's dogma on that evil, whereas Americans should be free of any legal enshrinement of such "sectarianism."

Few in favor of abortion maintain the laws against it were "sectarian" before the 1973 Supreme Court decision. Those laws simply carried on the unbroken tradition of law in the once-Christian West. They were enacted in most jurisdictions in this country when Catholic political influence was nearly non-existent and the Catholic electorate few in numbers.

It is only the attempt to return to a condition that existed before the virtual secularization of American culture that is called Catholic, an imposition of one Church's moral thought. (The Church does not determine the route of that return but most anti-abortionists are agreed a Constitutional amendment is the only possible way to end the Supreme Court's claim to dominate in the question.)

We need not be shocked if the same charge of sectarianism is made against all legal restrictions that prohibit what the new paganism may come to find acceptable. We already hear anti-pornography laws being attacked as the imposition of a moral viewpoint. Why should not laws against murder, rape, dueling, kidnapping, slavery, robbery, public nudity, child labor, prostitution, public sexual acts, pandering, providing narcotics, etc., be so faulted? All such laws coincide with Catholic dogma concerning the duty of government. They would become sectarian Catholicism should the public will come to accept them, something that is not beyond possibility at least for a number of such activities.

Is the public will sovereign, absolute? Is it the desire of the people—or even the vote of the people's representatives or the President's Supreme Court appointees—that is the true Leviathan, the possessor of all authority and the ultimate definer of all legality? If that is the case then we simply have absolutism by majority rule. Absolutism is any government's insistence it is answerable to no law outside itself and its determination. It is a necessary condition—mitigated only accidentally—for pagan civilizations all of which ended in absolutism.

The truth is that authority and law come from God. The application of authority and the enactment of law must be in keeping with God's will, the only absolute. All of Western civilization until most recently recognized that will in regard to the inviolability of innocent life. That vision faded with the triumph of outrageous ideas of "liberty," with false ideas of government, with a confusion about "rights"—what they are, from whence they originate, and who has them. But it has not faded from the Catholic Church, faithful to God's revelation and sensitive to the law known in God's creation. Abortion is devastatingly un-natural, and as such cannot be legalized, anymore than anarchy, or the absence of government can be legalized. In fact, abortion *is* anarchy at the most sensitive and vital point of human society.

A somewhat similar understanding is indicated

in this statement by Lon L. Fuller, Carter Professor of General Jurisprudence at Harvard Law School: "There never was a time that could reveal more plainly the vacuity of the view that law simply expresses a datum of legitimated social power. Nor was there ever a time when it was more dangerous to take that view seriously" (*The Morality of Law,* Yale University Press, 1964). The 1973 Supreme Court decision prohibiting most restrictions on abortion is based squarely on the idea that law is that datum of legitimated social power. There is no other basis—certainly none in morality or any concept of a natural law—upon which it could be based.

What, however, of the argument that abortion cannot pragmatically be prevented? Law against it is unenforceable, this argument goes. That is easily asserted concerning abortion, because a terrible stigma of shame was attached to it—and hence a sort of loathsome secrecy beyond that concerning other crimes—before its recent "legalization." It is easy in such circumstances to claim abortion was rampant even though outlawed.

That would hardly explain why, when certain jurisdictions and nations first legalized abortion they were swamped with candidates for abortion coming from places where it was still illegal. For the most part these were women who would

91

never have sought out illegal abortion—whether because of its risk or expense or the repulsiveness of the environment surrounding the slaying of the unborn. Abortion's very illegality meant few persons were available to do it—certainly not respectable physicians.

And the lament about abortion's denial to the poor by withholding welfare funds for that purpose is proof itself that law—which denies the possibility of free abortions—does curtail the evil. (Some will claim that very fact means we must legalize it, since the rich can obtain it in any case. Apply the same reasoning to murder, and we would have a situation wherein a poor man should have public subsidy to hire a hit man, since such services are available to the rich.)

The argument of unenforceability, of course, should not be a conclusive one, for though it may be that positive, man-made law becomes a non-law because of neglect of enforcement or inability to enforce, the same cannot be said of law required by the very nature of government and the nature of the human person and human rights.

Were murder to occur every minute (as perhaps it almost does) in the shadows of every alley, because people successfully defied the legal ban on murder, no government could validly remove from the statutes laws against murder.

Frank Morriss

Were our return to paganism to invite the practice of rape as a man's very right, an expression of machismo and the proper use of his body, no government should dare remove from the books laws preventing rape.

It is strange, indeed, that something worse than rape is now legally allowed as an expression of a woman's feministic "right," the free use of her body, though the victim is a child and dies without defender, public or private. If the state does not make laws against murder and rape non-law, and could not do so, why should it make laws against abortion non-laws?

The truth is that the government, for its own survival and good, is required to prohibit such immoralities as impinge upon the common good and endanger the safety, dignity—or with abortion, the very survival of countless citizens. A government that fails to have such laws enacted, with whatever enforcement of them is possible, denies its purpose and subverts its own authority. Human nature cannot accept a state of affairs in which the state allows a blood feud against a whole class of persons. If a nation cannot long endure half-slave and half-free, it certainly cannot long survive part-executioner, part-victim. And a government is required to seek its own perpetuation, because it is a necessary and required institution. Suicide for government is as

93

immoral as for an individual. Failure to protect the unborn is a step toward that suicide, for it is a denial of a governmental responsibility.

It is apparent that those who believe a law against abortion is "Constantinism" do not feel the same is the case of laws against slavery, laws against child labor or monopoly, or laws guarding the right to organize, etc. Yet those are as clearly upheld by Catholic doctrine as is law prohibiting abortion. And, indeed, it is only Catholic doctrine that demands them as morally and metaphysically necessary in a proper functioning society. For others they are merely the result of political or judicial power.

Can the truth be that those willing to have such social legislation, even when it is called for by Catholic doctrine, do so because it favors a vocal constituency? Catholic doctrine against abortion, however, favors the rights of a voiceless, voteless class of humans. Invoking the idea that the call for a prohibition of abortion is an improper reliance on civil power to enforce Catholic doctrine in a pluralistic society can well be defensive sophistry to justify abandonment of the rights of the silent unborn.

There is a tendency to carry the legitimate separation of Church and State so far as to deny that it is within the Church's power to interpret the natural law and call for its application. Such a view is Caesarism, as asserted by the anti-Papal Bourbons and later nationalistic reformers such as Cranmer and their creatures; the early Stuart kings; and finally by the British rulers from whom Americans broke.

"Let the Church be silent," is the cry. And some Catholics, perhaps embarrassed at what they understand (often without historical knowledge) to have been abuses in the past, not only echo the cry but maintain that the Catholic citizen should not seek the application in society and law of anything that contains a moral content, especially when the Church alone holds to it.

That is not the teaching of Vatican II: "Christ did not bequeath to the Church a mission in the political, economic or social order; the purpose He assigned to it was a religious one. But this religious mission can be the source of commitment, direction, and vigor to establish and consolidate the community of men according to the law of God. In fact, the Church is able, indeed is obliged, if times and circumstances require it, to initiate action for the benefit of all men, especially those in need, like works of mercy and similar undertakings" (*Gaudium et Spes,* IV, 42).

Lest anyone consider such works limited to mere private effort in the private realm consider what the Council says here: " . . . Political authority, either within the political community as such or through organizations representing the state must be exercised within the limits of the moral order and directed toward the common good (understood in the dynamic sense of the term) according to the juridical order legitimately established or due to be established . . ." (*Gaudium et Spes,* IV, 74).

Though the Church does not enter politics today in the person of its leaders and officers, it sees the pertinent influence of the moral and natural law through its members in every nation: "Those with a talent for the difficult yet noble art of politics, or whose talents in this matter can be developed, should prepare themselves for it, and, forgetting their own convenience and material interests, they should engage in political activity. They must combat injustice and oppression, arbitrary domination and intolerance by individuals or political parties . . ." (*Gaudium et Spes,* IV, 75).

There is no greater injustice than abortion, because it is ultimate and irremedial injustice. There is no greater oppression to be fought than that of unborn children, who are without tongue to defend themselves. That the Church calls its faithful under every government—democratic or dictatorial—to seek legal redress of this injustice is beyond real question.

Consider this statement by the brilliant Pope Pius XII: "The power of the Church is not bound by the limits of 'matters strictly religious,' as they say, but the whole matter of the natural law, its foundation, its interpretation, its application, so far as their moral aspects extend, are within the Church's power" (Address Nov. 2, 1954, in celebration of the dogma of the Assumption).

In the same address, Pope Pius XII quoted from the monumental letter *Singulari Quandam* of St. Pius X: "Whatever a Christian man may do, even in affairs of this world, he may not ignore the supernatural; nay, he must direct all to the highest good as his last end, in accordance with the dictates of Christian wisdom."

Christian wisdom commends the crusade to end abortion, as far as it can be ended, by appeal to law, which is the civil and divine guardian of the right of mankind to pursue that proper end spoken of by St. Pius X.

Does the Church's Stand Contradict
True Americanism?

Even educated Americans have rarely been taught true history about either the origins or nature of liberty, the theories of government that have obtained over the centuries, and the Church's role in combatting absolutism. The Church in fact has been the victim of a great lie that links it to the tyranny of kings and nobility, whereas, in fact, individual rights found their greatest defender in the Church.

The Church has always insisted that there were boundaries that prevented the state's invasion of Church rights and the rights of citizens and subjects. That was the burden of Magna Carta, drafted by Churchmen and Catholic barons against a Plantagenet monarch who had an exaggerated concept of a ruler's powers.

The Church battled the absolutist pretensions of the Holy Roman Emperors, the French monarchs, the Tudors—just as it today battles such pretensions held by dictators of Left or Right. The reason is that the Church knows that authority comes from God; so do rights. The authority of rulers cannot contradict or abrogate rights.

If, however, we must accept abortion because the

majority of a nine-man court says we should—whereas God's law clearly says we shouldn't and indeed tells rulers they must protect all humans equally—then we have invested that court with absolutist power. We have said that law is what some judges declare it to be, whereas the true concept of a Supreme Court is that it is supreme only in its mandate to find what the law is and proclaim it. All remedies available against absolutism must be sought. The only one available—short of revolution—is a Constitutional amendment incorporating a truth of the Natural Law as supreme above the contention of the Court.

That is certainly every bit as American as the Founding Fathers' appeal to king, Parliament and finally to the "laws of Nature and of Nature's God." They had not yet a Constitution to embody that phrase. Significantly, they put it in the same Declaration which complained of the King's failure to enact laws protective of Americans, who were in a sense citizens in the womb of history.

Unfortunately, the concept of the origin of human rights has faded almost out of sight, so that the very soul of the American Revolution can rightly be called all but dead. First, the notion of Hobbes' Leviathan, wreathed and garlanded and masqued by Rousseau, invaded the American mind. All powers and rights are surrendered—not crudely to a man as Hobbes had it—but to the common will, the majority vote.

Still, the idea of natural law and the living role of precedent prevailed in our jurisprudence roughly until the triumph of the positivistic school represented by Oliver Wendell Holmes, Jr., who said the prayerbook was a mystery he never touched. Once again government became absolutist. Law was what the state said it was—and when Holmes said state, he meant the Court on which he served. A right then became "the hypostasis of a prophecy"—what the future would accept. How? By general will.

It is a result of that type of reasoning that brought about the abortion decision of 1973 calling abortion a woman's "right" and prohibiting most restrictions of it. The same reasoning dictates an acceptance of the decision, regardless of one's personal view about abortion. Laws thereby becomes decision or ukase, rather than authority and force exercised in behalf of rights and the common good, all measured by human nature rather than human inclination.

The Church in objecting to this actually speaks in conformity with the true American Revolution, freed from the musings of Rousseau and the mistake of Locke about government resulting from a man-made compact.

It should be noted that Vatican II's condemnation of abortion as criminal and poisonous of civilization comes in a section discussing respect for the human person. Liberty must involve such respect; license never does. The liberty to kill respects power, a priority of birth, the desire for unencumbrance—but it does not respect the human person, since it almost inevitably destroys the life of such a person. Nor does it even respect the person of the woman choosing abortion, for that choice degrades the mother, beckoning her to something against her own vocation and fulfillment, and involving her in a guilt from which she will never escape.

Unfortunately—but inevitably—atheistic existentialism has joined hands with the new absolutism to invest in some a so-called right to choose the death of another innocent person. Lurking within this decision is the existential idea that choice itself is good, without reference to the object or act chosen. It is a sort of self-deification, a defiance of the author of will by its exercise against His law.

God has willed that there be life; we challenge God by claiming the right to will that there be death, and we back up the challenge with the power we have to kill. Civilization has had many ancient and ugly words for the exercise of such power—assassination, infanticide, homicide, murder, or an "ultimate solution."

We do in fact choose "homicide" to describe abortion, since that leaves the good will or intention of the perpetrators aside. We do not judge them, nor is it necessary. Let us by law—as demanded by every way of measure, propriety, congruity, sanity—prevent such homicides, putting all whether of good will or ill on notice that all homicides of the innocent cannot be tolerated.

Let no generation of the future indict us for a holocaust that consumed our fellow humans under the excuse that some could use the term "unwanted" as a warrant for liquidation. If Pope Pius XI should be applauded for condemning the immoralities of Naziism in the encyclical *Mit Brennender Sorge,* surely the Church today can only be applauded for condemning the immorality—and inhumanity—of abortion.

WHAT OF THE AMERICAN RIGHT
OF FREE CHOICE?

One major purpose of law is to limit the right of free choice. Obviously we do not leave it a free choice as to what speed one should drive, of whether one should pay income tax or not, or whether one should have one wife or a dozen. Are such things regulated by law only because a majority feel they should be, or because they are for the common good, necessary for the proper working of government and society? Could a majority vote or a legal decision really make "legal" much less moral the right to choose to drive 100 miles an hour through a school zone when children were being sent home?

Law cannot exist to protect "the right to choose" when a possible choice may irreparably harm others, or else we would not have restraining orders, injunctions, or any other law or judicial instrument against invading rights, property, or actions of others. Nor can it protect any right to choose an action against the common good, against the rights protected by the Constitution.

Yes, the Supreme Court has avoided the 14th Amendment in regard to the life of the unborn by simply declaring the unborn, in effect, non-persons, at least for the purpose of allowing them to be aborted. It is still, however, perfectly proper and truly American to override that decision by amending the Constitution to include the unborn under such protection, or to effect their protection in any way the people desire. Failure to pass such an amendment does not make the Supreme Court decision good law, for there is a higher law that estops a court from letting down the barriers of protection for all persons. At the moment the common good calls for opposition to that Supreme Court decision through the Constitutionally established procedures of amendment.

To say it is not good Americanism to seek a Constitutional amendment against abortion is to say it is not good Americanism to follow the Constitution itself. That is patent absurdity.

As suggested elsewhere, we would never have had legal abortion if the beliefs and legal understanding of the Founding Fathers had prevailed. Had, for example, George Mason, author of the Bill of Rights, foreseen "legal" abortion, he certainly would have used that Bill of Rights to prohibit it, for he considered such a document the final protector of basic rights. The truly un-American thing is that the Supreme Court has become in effect an absolutist body, creating law rather than interpreting it, claiming to bestow rights rather than guarding them, and favoring one class of persons against another.

The latter the pro-abortion Justices had to do—for if they wanted to grant the "right" of abortion in any condition of fairness, they would have had to recognize the right of physicians to take deadly action against mothers, at, let us say, the behest of husbands, or perhaps of children already born. If relationship (motherhood) gives a right to kill, then why doesn't other relationship give the same.

Instead, the Court has led us into the field of incongruity, a Wonderland where an unborn may be considered a person in tort law but a nonperson in regard to the right to live; where an unborn can get life-saving medical treatment at the decision of its parents, but can be doomed to death at a mother's whim, with the father having no right to be heard; where doctors can be hired to kill the child in the womb, but be required by law to treat it should that homicidal effort fail.

Respect for law in such conditions becomes impossible, and the result we see growing each day—the idea that the only crime is in getting caught. If you excuse something the heart knows is criminal, you lose the authority to call anything else wrong.

APPENDIX

Citations Pertinent to the Church's Condem-
nation of Abortion and the Duty of the State in
That Regard

SCRIPTURE

"The Lord answered Isaac and his wife
Rebecca conceived. The children jostled each
other within her. . . ."

Gen. XV: 22

". . . Or why was I not buried away like an un-
timely birth, like babes that have never seen the
light

Job iii: 16

"Behold, sons are a gift from the Lord; the
fruit of the womb is a reward. . . ."

Psalm 126

"The word of the Lord came to me thus:
Before I formed you in the womb I knew you,
before you were born I dedicated you, a prophet
to the nations I appointed you."

Jer. I, 4-6

"Blessed art thou among women and blessed is the fruit of thy womb!"

Luke I: 42

"For behold, the moment that the sound of thy greeting came to my ears, the babe in my womb leapt for joy."

Luke I: 43

"When Mary his mother had been betrothed to Joseph, before they came together, she was found to be with child by the Holy Spirit.

Matt. I: 18

ANCIENT SCIENCE

". . . I will not give to a woman an abortifacient pessary. In purity and holiness I will guard my life and my art."

Oath ascribed to Hippocrates B.C. 460-339

MODERN SCIENCE

"Karl Ernest von Baer in 1827 had discovered the ovum in the human female; by 1875 the joint action of spermatozoon and ovum in gerenation had been determined. A change in organism was seen to occur at the moment of fertilization which distinguished the resultant from the components. . . . If a moment had to be chosen for ensoulment, no convincing argument now appeared to support Aristotle or to put ensoulment at a late stage of fetal life.''

John T. Noonan, Jr.,
The Morality of Abortion
Harvard University Press, 1970, p. 38

". . . When people want to discard a baby they say to you that it is not yet a baby. It's something which is not that. And they try to build a theory of 'humanization,' saying that in the beginning there is something which is living, something which is maybe a little human, but it is not a human being, and it is with the improvement of it that some day, by a humanization process, it will become a true human fellow.

"Well, that's curious, because nobody argues about that when we are dealing with mice, for example, or when we are dealing with cattle, or even when we are dealing with a big primate like the chimpanzee. Nobody believes that there is a progressive chimpanzification of a chimpanzee. Nobody believes that there is a progressive cattlization of tiny cattle. Why then does he believe that there is a progressive humanization of a human being? For a very simple reason. Because it doesn't matter the size of the chimpanzee you kill, you are sure you are killing just a chimpanzee. Well, it's not very nice to kill chimpanzees—I don't like that. But it is not so important as to kill one member of our species.

"But when you are dealing with human beings that you want to destroy, it is difficult to accept that they are similar to you. Then you get into moral trouble. And that is just the reason why people try to masquerade the truth by asking questions which have no sense. Because they would not scientifically ask those questions for any other living system than the system they will to destroy."

> Prof. Jerome Lejeune, holder of the chair of Fundamental Genetics, the University of Paris, in an address at the fourth combined conference of the Quality of Life, sponsored by the Guild of St. Luke, Ss. Cosmas and Damian of Aukland-Wellington, at Wairakei, N.Z., Oct. 9-12, 1975.

"In this Orwellian situation, where so much semantic effort and logical gymnastics are expended in making a developing human into an 'un-person,' modern anatomical, genetic, immunological, endocrinological and physiological facts are a persistent embarrassment. How much easier to echo that simple statement, 'But there's

110

nothing there yet,' without pausing to reflect that if there is nothing there, then why the unholy rush to remove it?''

> Sir William Liley, KCMG, Ph.D., B.Sc. (Hon), M.B. Ch.B., B.Med,Sc., Dip.Obst, F.R.S.N.Z, F.R.C.O.G, F.A.C.O.G, professor of perinatal physicology in the postgraduate school of obstetrics and gynaecology, Auckland, speaking at the Wairakei conference, 1975.

"We know that he (the unborn) moves with a delightful easy grace in his buoyant world, that foetal comfort determines foetal position. He is responsive to pain and touch and cold and sound and light. He drinks his amniotic fluid, more if it is artificially sweetened, less if it is given an unpleasant taste. He gets hiccups and sucks his thumb. He wakes and sleeps. He gets bored with repetitive signals but can be taught to be alerted by a first signal for a second different one. And finally he determines his birthday, for unquestionably the onset of labour is a unilateral decision of the foetus.

"This then is the foetus we know and indeed we each once were. This is the foetus we look after in modern obstetrics, the same baby we are caring for before and after birth, who before birth can be ill and need diagnosis and treatment just like any other patient.''

> Dr. Liley, *Liberal Studies,* ''A Case Against Abortion,'' Whitcombe & Tombs, Ltd., 1971, as quoted in *Handbook on Abortion,* by Dr. and Mrs. J. C. Wilke, Hiltz Co., Cincinnati, Ohio, 1971.

PHILOSOPHY

''Every being, however, above the level of brute animality is styled a person. Every human being is a 'person,' irrespective of age, sex, color, or condition. A child, even though unborn, is a 'person' in the strict sense of the term, and the courts of law recognize it as a potential heir to an estate.''

> Celestine N. Bittle, O.M.Cap., *The Domain of Being,* Bruce, Milwaukee, 1939, p. 268.

''For a person, clearly, is nothing else than an individual substance possessed of rational nature.''

> St. Thomas Aquinas, *Compendium of Theology,* trans. Cyril Vollet, S.J., S.T.D.;B. Herder, St. Louis, 1947, p. 230.

HISTORY

"You shall not slay the child by abortions (*phthora*). You shall not kill what is generated."

> The *Didache (Teaching of the Twelve Apostles),* 2:2.

"How can we kill a man when we are those who say that all who use abortifacients are homicides and will account to God for their abortions as for the killing of men. For the fetus in the womb is not an animal, and it is God's providence that he exists."

> Athenagoras, *Patrologia graeca,* 6, 919, answering charges that Christians practiced cannibalism.

"The offspring of 'hereditarily diseased persons' who had slipped through the sterilization net could be legally aborted (as could embryos reputed to be half-Jewish) although abortion *per se* was one of the most heinous crimes in the Nazi statute book."

> *The 12-Year Reich,* by Richard Grunberger, Holt, Rinehard and Winston, N.Y., 1971. p. 238.

(A footnote to the reference to abortion of "hereditarily diseased persons" is this: "This required the approval of three doctors as well as the mother's consent. . . ." The "sterilization net" mentioned in Mr. Grunberger's book was for Germans suffering from physical malformation, mental retardation, epilepsy, imbecility, deafness or blindness. Such sterilization was mandatory, but was backed up by legal abortion.)

THE MAGISTERIUM

Propositions condemned by the Holy Office, March 2, 1679:

"34. It is lawful to procure abortion before ensoulment of the fetus, lest a girl, detected as pregnant, be killed or defamed.

"35. It seems probable that the fetus (as long as it is in the uterus, lacks a rational soul and begins first to have one when it is born; and consequently it must be said that no abortion is homicide."

(Stating the penalty of excommunication for abortion, Pope Pius IX in 1869—*Apostolicace sedis*—removed any mention of earlier penalties concerning "ensoulment."

* * *

"What cause can ever avail to excuse in any way the direct killing of the innocent? For it is a question of that. Whether it is inflicted on